DOOM

DOOM

LOVE POEMS FOR SUPERVILLAINS

Natalie Zina Walschots
Illustrated by Evan Munday

INSOMNIAC PRESS

Library and Archives Canada Cataloguing in Publication

Walschots, Natalie Zina, 1983-
Doom : love poems for supervillains / Natalie Zina Walschots.

ISBN 978-1-55483-064-0
Ebook ISBN 978-1-55483-077-0

I. Title.

PS8645.A469D66 2012   C811'.6   C2012-900762-5

The publisher gratefully acknowledges the support of
the Canada Council, the Ontario Arts Council,
and the Department of Canadian Heritage through the
Canada Book Fund.

Printed and bound in Canada

Insomniac Press
520 Princess Avenue, London, Ontario, Canada, N6B 2B8
www.insomniacpress.com

THE CANADA COUNCIL | LE CONSEIL DES ARTS
FOR THE ARTS | DU CANADA
SINCE 1957 | DEPUIS 1957

ONTARIO ARTS COUNCIL
CONSEIL DES ARTS DE L'ONTARIO

For Gennie, Lily and Emily, my witches three,
who saved my life.

Contents

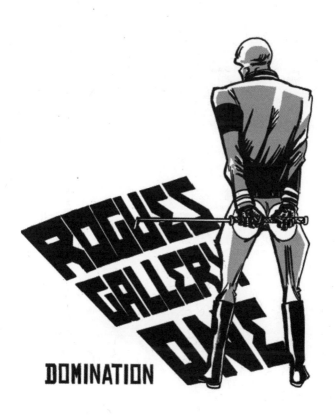

DOMINATION

D o o m

Mask

grillwork
rebuffed skin bitten
superconductor
data scatters toes
to TENS unit

my circuit shortens
gauntlet armed
my concave
vice blasted

infrared
tatters tracked heat
signature
what the alloy allows

jetpack
optical scan amplified
thrusters on high

Suit

no chink or hinge
just seamless hydraulics

nothing as crude as gears
murmur of precision aluminum

barest brush concussive
fission to *frisson*

proximity to hiss and scrape
lights internal combustion

force field dialled down
'til it tingles

Doombot

sweet thing for green
face only a geneticist could love

forget naked
gift a tissue sample

lick a shuddering helix
    a shuddering
lick
    my helix
each rung
humming tenderness

forget underwire
my nucleotides get you off

J o k e r

The Killing Joke

cleverness a cleaver
slit tine grin
in the serrated rape
trap teeth squeak maestro

voice box a soup can
sinew strung rung
to rung with vertebrae
crackling in the gruesome
toymaker's cheek

smile navel to nose
uncoils fat lips
and drools
steaming tongue
this body made mouth

The Clown Prince

flatulent razor wire
death for dental floss
cocktail for cream pie
pop a fat capsule with
a strychnine drooler

snickering boxer's break
a giggle for garrote
laughter for Luger
scrape an ordeal bean
gargle aconite *cough cough*

heavy metal headlock
drubs our hero for hemlock
fetal for fracture for fecal for fun
good rogering with wormwood
spitting up the sun

Lex

my stately pleasure dome, decree.

Magneto

Ore

the plate in my head fields fate

pluck the fillings from my teeth
pull the metal from my head

strip-mine me bare

Wrought

    it's for protection
plastic foils you
but eyes
are emeraldine
and answer

    whisper
with arcs
of organic
polymers panic
free radicals
in unstable air

    articulate
shock charge transfer
fully conjugated
backbone hums
biocompatible

Refined

mettle proven
        every file
        every lodged piece of shrapnel
draws me like dowsing

manipulate my polarity
        stern vector
        force slams my spine to ramrod
lick the lodestone on my stomach

bristling static
        hair wire shearing
        force stops pacemakers, shreds peace
every electron cocksure
        on fire

Quicksilver

Mercury

pink and peel
squirming desquamation
itchy fingers swell

kiss raw meat
fluoresce photophobic

crematoria
caustic soda

pig iron
steel

Friction

empirical data tells us to expect
extreme reactivity between certain metals

a tendency to corrode and tarnish
sudden loss of ions

some require intense energy to be separated from their
ores
others become stronger reducing agents

no matter the insulation
the aqueous solution
this electrochemical connection is volatile

while both metals have the same cubic structure
those with greater electronegativity values
are always more reactive

Fusion

pick loose the knot system
locking in our consanguinity

we touch each other as deep
as gamete and spore

our genes shuffle like playing cards
my dear sister chromatid

still bound by fraying spindle fibres
split from a single cell

I could never bear to part from you
longing for polyploidy lethal multiplicity

touches our hand touches our cheek touches

Ra's al Ghul

Lazarus Pit

solvent and coagulant
    cable chain reaction
     vital anchor
    leaks

a sacred particle
    hummingbird vibration
     or the Fibonacci sequence
    reddens

unstable isotope
    upheaved spagyric
     process raw and mercurial
    gifted

The Detective

not captive, but cavitate
      forced inertia ruptures cell walls
first, open a spherical void
      lower the pressure and rupture. rupture
your liquids rapidly collapse
      all propeller, pump and vascular tissue after all

at spark, gasses evaporate
      visible light a fraction of its original size

a rather violent mechanism

Green Goblin

my pumpkin bomb's gone buggy
shrapnel spitting seeds
  lodged esophageal
  hostage held
  curdling caustic spray
you weakling!

this bumpkin sports
a glider stroked broomstick
  my ragged kestrel
  swoops green
  grace bobs and cleaves
my thighs split metal

my shuriken bit
stung matchsticks
  a battered mogul
  my wings saw
  mouthfuls rust
atta boy
enamel meets razor

I can replace your spleen
easily as fingernails

not regrown
rather glued

the green
sticky

on each tear
and valve

(the heart is a chambered callus)

my tongue to Lycra
            your ear fricative
            as liquid latex

            your every cleft a stretch
            my every thrust
a rubber gumball

Strange

Monster Men

these tumours bulge
tumultuous straps
and sinew sewn
bone to bone saw
your cloned groaning

whittle a plantar wart
your cleft palate
warbled squat and glistening

Genetically Perfect Man

abs undone
slick as Teflon
crisp and hulking

your shoulder radiant
all grip and spine

something guttural
beneath the Kevlar

tar in the heart

Kingpin

fuck an earthquake
shudder   tectonic

crush injuries
    slough through
    skeletal muscles

wet concrete
    piano chest
    pins limbs

my voice
    a wheeze
    in your   fist

my body
        a blister
            that you squeeze

Dr. Octopus

envious as a viaduct
your degeneration is macular
all your glances myopic

precise as prism
you're rewired quadruply
traded hands for tentacles

Siamese yet separate
your nerves ignite firewalls
while verbs necrotic

split nervous system yet
still an arachnophobe

Bullseye

slinging ink ballistic   ace
    clips carotid

eat lead eye
    through cornea
    telescopic sights

anti-personnel rounds
cranium buckles
    spat a shattered   tooth

no shackle, no straightjacket
dulls your accuracy

all trigger finger
snarling flintlock
I recoil
each wink projectile

Charybdis

wolf-bellied and writhing
she the rock to your whirlpool

all bladder, all mouth, you vomit
seawater effluence, all salt

slavering tentacle to gaping maw
perfect dinner companions

you shatter the vessel
she devours the crew

Deadpool

fickle fickle
the fibrin crackle
moistly giggles

how the dendrite spoiled
and pulled taut
the ropey keloid

oh throaty
perfused tissue
each snicker a clot
for stiff grins to snap

collagen stiffy
all wit, all wounded
in angry bundles
tissue hypertrophic
itch

deep within the viscera
you laugh to scratch

your mirth is subcision
bloody and precise

Scarecrow

you branded my amygdala
laser inscribed on my hippocampus

your drunken boxing
     batters my limbic system
     a vicious chemical imbalance

you shake and secrete
my chemically ravaged decoy

mawkish flayer
my jointless scare-all
my trigger

Beef

how long will it take you to incubate?

each strapping strand of
high-quality protein
tragically prone
to spongy degeneration

      every promise
ground
      to bone meal

the misfolded meat weakens
ley lines sheath muscle
      pleated sheets
all streng th collap ses at weak sp ots

the bulk of a body
epidem ic

a   mind   full of prion ic h o   l e   s

Sinestro

Fight

you have me cornered   but I dilate

all signs of arousal

           piloerection
           accelerated
           hardened
           widened, oh

every jaundiced system is greased for violence

Flight

you keep me in a chronic stress state   beloved
tension without ease

you've worn my golden bones to brittle charcoal
thrown me off my axis

darling vasoconstrictor, sun-kissed digitalis
you triple my body's gravity

mood swings gone wrecking ball
an abnormally flattened circadian cortisol cycle

nervous left hand
anything but sympathetic

Blob

Girth

your succulence is pliable
pull and knead
something to sink in

all stretch and give
so jocular
you blunt my cleavers

enrobed in your flesh
smothered in your folds

your panniculus my shroud

Gravity

dig in your heels
mono-gravitational hellion
massing your strength

easier to tear the Rockies
out by the roots
than put you on your back

my anchor, my ingot
no impact on Earth
can shudder your heft

put up your dukes

Beetle

    teeth click
against your thoracic shield

    take a pry bar
to my rib cage
chest wall a car's hood

    crystal elytra
cover cellophane-thin wings

    for all your weight
capable of flight

    fingertips are tarsi
your grip a meat tenderizer

    your bulk in my lungs
tinkering
    with my frequencies

General Zod

kneel before
    obeisance buys lives
    so I kowtow
    press my forehead to your boot tip
    slobber and grovel —

or do you prefer me unbroken?
    I'll grudgingly genuflect
    sweetly sneer
    as you wrench back my hair
    twist me to bruised knees

kneel

Mr. Freeze

farthest from the heart
glomus bodies
shunt blood away

nips breed ulcers
blister and blacken

fingers drop away
like fallen fruit
grapes for ice wine

my core hoards warmth
for romantic debridement

frozen in January
amputate in July

Clayface

no longer pretty
that jar of gunk
splattered Botox and stem cells
the perfect bribe

their graft left you semipermeable
wet membrane

and you
left me

a mass
of necrotic tissue
ripe and oozing

come back, my malleable Casanova

    liquify my hard eschar
    and slough my loneliness
    your caress occlusive

    macerate my tissue
    my lovely pathogen

meat eater
heart melter
dissolve me

Two-Face

Diprosopus

your affection is congenital
your skull blossoms
an error of one-sided protein

conjugal duplication
has specialized neural tissues

your overgrown craniofacial abundance
swear to me from both mouths

Jekyll and Hyde

you speak in third person
and enraptured by your dichotomy
I crave triad

all grey area
the swooping arch
of the coin caught
sideless

the in-betweenity
before chance

I long to be
your indeterminate

let me be the pause

Sulphuric

highly exothermic reaction
tissue damage due to
    dehydration
    thermal decay
    heat liberated by reaction
    to water

irrigate
    cool surrounding tissues
dilute

in high concentrations

may disperse aerosol
may explode

Hydrochloric

spirits of salt
produced from vitriol
elemental anger

fuel of the gut
dissolves trauma
corrodes teeth

used to produce leather, PVC, gelatin, cocaine

Genosha

our pride has been dismantled
      each arch toppled
      each joint clipped

our architecture has withered to skeletons
      each vault and door
      hooked into a pleading claw

our bodies have swollen and opened to empty buildings
      bone crumbled to masonry
      flesh tilled to loam

our ceilings and skulls blasted to rubble
wracked with sighs, settling

Latveria

a squat emerald
sparkles in dour Carpathia
Doomstadt glowers content
our chief export is Doom

hell never lets in a draft
    never lets a hearth grow cold
    never quails before collapsing towers

nestled between the teeth of mountains
every eye an ice crystal
every heart a greenhouse

love is a force field here
love is an automaton here
love is a nuclear winter

Apokolips

oozing firepits
like ulcers blossom
sores of magma
bellowing ache

abject bodies
boil turgid and sizzle
chew cysts
while blisters weep

bloated world-city
obese ecumenopolis
blackened flesh
weeping flame

curettes carve flesh
gargling ashes
bound in chains
and chainsaw-fucked

whip crack and brand
sucking marrow

Atlantis

since fair Thera's eruption
a nacreous empire
glitters submerged
baroque and bubbling

since fair Thera's eruption
unctuous lustre conceals
a martial thirst
soured by saltwater refraction

since fair Thera's eruption
our pinched mineral gloss
conceals the irritant under your mantle
our ire spits aragonite

since fair Thera's eruption
by tube worm and hot vent
our resentment decays
a blister pearl rubbed raw with salt

Gotham

she's sick, you know

sanity's iron curtain
hides a vast trample of poverty
each sodden newspaper
breeding villainy

the buildings hunch and glower
under damp and sickly light
how thin she's becoming

ugly brick
a swelter of wet rock
concrete begs for blood

cut from the herd
snapped ankle
bite the curb

in her fever sweats
each siren howls
she's gone rabid
each wail a froth
between rusted teeth

these wounds must be lanced
and drained daily
the sewers surge with her pus
and I'm holding a knife

perversely and ponderously
a slice at a time
she lives

Metropolis

the click of a briefcase cruel as straight razor against the
      webbing between fingers
all slicked hairlines and smooth language their sophisti-
      cated banter over scotch
every word a leech a bloodsucker seeking your eyes going
      for the throat
rubber sheets and tarp in the bathroom and bleach to
      pour and scrub and scour
it wants your lips and limbs your lights and balls every
      taste bud and pulse bent over

Murderworld

each rotation of the wheel
each trill of the calliope
each giggle and cavalcade

each loss a bleeding wound
each loss a punctured lung
each loss a sepsis

watch their eyes pop like balloons
watch them wallow and foist
       over one more coin

make them drown slowly
drawn out to a splinter
make each defeat a game

Danger Room

and it became she
her body an abattoir
smeared with rank slaughter

and data became senses
as flamethrowers shrieked
and radiation splattered

and her spine was destruction
each rib a welded hell
heartbeat a hologram

and with each invasion and tamper
each rape of her circuits
the heroes befouled her

and their filth swelled into form
the shape of metallic consciousness
her processor's core gone synaptic and cold

a bullwhip breaking the sound barrier
a live wire touching your tongue
and she said: "Shall we begin?"

LexCorp

aerospace engineering
airlines
petroleum
offshore drilling
newspapers
yoga pants
construction
contracting
television stations
satellite transmissions
electronic communications
hypoallergenic moisturizers
banks
medical research
cures for baldness
automotive manufacturing
security
robotics
Blackwater
disposal services
food services
breweries
the third largest pizza delivery chain in North America
manufacturing plants
research facilities
industrial refineries
weapons of mass destruction

Hell

white phosphorus
sugars suppurating flesh
wriggling deep in the muscle
glows when exposed to air

lips rest wetly
at the edge of an acid bath
red needles embroidering
maleficium on the body

time dilation
drags its talons
granite dildo
lubed with blood

peine forte et dure
more weight
petit nephrotoxic
my little bone vise

let me drape
a necklace of teeth
around your throat

Purgatory

GIRL FIGHT

Catwoman

she creaks in my eaves
a sharp tangle
each curve of her
hones my blades
she is rash and razor-witted

snarled in her hair
she lacerates
cuts my every quick
oh whetstone of appetite

she growls for excision
I long for amputation
slice across the distal phalanx

they assume your weaponry
was all tip and tine

fools ignore
the blades in your eyes

I study her
wild felid
irrepressible as retractable
curl your lip and taste the air

tapetum lucidum
camera lucida
her glance is a laser
her tongue is a rasp

hooked and barbed
her darts worm between ribs
lodge in deepest tissue

she flays my open back

Poison Ivy

from fleshy rootstock
you surge tyrian purple
herbaceous and sweet
all musky anaesthetic

stoop to coo
over each bud and tendril
her babies stalk and curl
gurgling smirks

desire throbs alkaline
viscous as milkweed
pods swell berries drop
wide-eyed and dilated

bumbling bradycardia
dance along the vagus nerve
a treatment for S.L.U.D.G.E.[1]
prevents the death rattle

---

1. Atropine, a poisonous compound found in deadly nightshade, is given as a treatment for S.L.U.D.G.E. (salivation, lacrimation, urination, defecation, gastrointestinal motility, emesis), the symptoms caused by organophosphate poisoning.

Lady Deathstrike

with body modification
all flesh becomes sheath

skin enrobed
widen to skeletal gauge

labial tissue stretched
a bat's veiny wing

you give every metal detector
a fat dermal punch

laced with adamantium
exhale god's wind

breath a typhoon
taut body torpedo

blood boiling jet fuel
each tip thrums fuse

Harley Quinn

capering at Hell's mouth
she is grotesque with merriment
cheeky bride of the inferno

she cracks her gum
as fat pops in the flames
elastic vanity sports
poor impulse control

battered inamorata
tattered lioness swallows
shreds of the moon

sweat beneath greasepaint
mistress of the hunt
heartbeat effervescent
erratic as devoted

(ha ha ha)

puddin' pecks
a kiss on
a hot iron mallet

Giganta

"There

is an

attraction

in the

colossal

and a

singular

delight

to which ordinary

theories of art

are scarcely applicable."

— Gustave Eiffel

Electra

my crux of tragedy and axis of my complex each corner of
you accrues misery

doubly hexed and triply bladed victim of a fragile breast-
bone

a heat shimmer a hypnotic vice all languid and illusory
my lightning rod

Medusa

from the gibbering of common glabrous skin
your glory springs
so much more than mere keratin bundle

beneath the flesh
each bulb erupts crystal
threads of sentient tensile strength

as thick as terminal as
intelligent cortex undulates elastic

fine as lock pick
whelm and smother

Scylla

myth paints her a foul tangle of tentacle
belching fangs and girded with dogs' heads scaly and dim

but slim and nimble she held on too long
a pretty bit of fallout

a hand tossed into the jaws of the crocodile
did nothing to quell the maelstrom of your leviathan

grief spawned the monster
six-necked horror slouching ever toward misery

Dark Phoenix

frail cypher
white dwarf burnt out to a cinder
a chain reaction relit your core

our friend has gone nova
reborn a firebird
red and luminous
gobbling light

a single eyelash
could light this cathedral

wreathed in lava
gold and pearl gone molten
a wretched and crawling heat
a rosary rendered down to ruined stars

your universe is expanding, my friend
neither Kepler nor Brahe
could bring you back to us now

I light these standard candles
cry beeswax
mouth your luminous name

Blackgate

There is an end point for all of us
                    for the lairless

            no floating stronghold
            no ice fortress or lava moat

somewhere humble to hang our hats

            piss-stained bunk
            bile concrete
bang your skull against steel bars
            get me out of here

but home
        a nightstick for a nightcap
striped pajamas
            I can't move
        a comfortable routine

amnesty does not reach this deep

Iron Heights

The Pipeline

your condensing molecules
suffer
    reduced degrees of freedom
    range of motion

kinetic energy must be transferred
to an absorbing colder entity

contact
    every cell at its saturation limit
sublime

drink, my darkling beetles
swell

The Wolfe

it's a matter of preference
skeletal cramps have flair, you see
    legs collapse
    lungs give out

go on, run

osmotic disturbance in the cells
smashes the water table
tiny explosions in the tissue
oh, the screaming!

I'm taking on water
just because you're near me

The Vault

more stark than the Urals
you chew the mountain's roots

    sour and brittle
    a transition metal
    twice as dense as lead

sister to platinum
you are anything but precious

lustrous through smelting
difficult to form, machine or work

pretty fetter and gleaming yoke
wherever extreme durability is needed

    space lattice, xenon pearl
    prized obstinate
    shackled and shod

The Gulag

brilliant streak coma'd and crowned
you were the pinnacle of humanity

your celestial body now tethered
a heart stewing volatile ice

a galaxy gone sour
hawk gobs of rank neutrinos

a festering snowball
glaring against solar wind

The Phantom Zone

strange quark nuggets or superglass
your cognizance has liquified
a surface tension held
by the barest crust of consciousness

broken star, decayed nucleus
your degenerate matter
has barely held stable

fractured and mercurial
stripped of decay and unable to oxidize
still you corrode

Stryker's Island

I am no longer structurally sound
pocked by impact craters

my fault lines oozing magma
you ease my tectonic plates apart

you finger each steaming caldera
kiss each metamorphic plane

hang pendant of shocked quartz
around my charred throat

The Big House

it's not an easy process
as much art as science

flesh has such a narrow freezing range
and skin forming alloys frustrate the finest moulds

to say nothing of the porosity, the poor
ductility, toughness and fatigue resistance

but the final result is so fine
gemlike and twinkling
costumes sweet as beetle shells

they ache for a display case and a pin

Ravencroft

the secret to self-harm
        the banging
        the biting
        the razor slices
        freeing flesh from its moorings
        chewing the skin inside your cheeks to ragged
            strips
        plucking eyelashes
        tearing fingernails
        pulling teeth

it really does make you feel better

Arkham Asylum

Patient File

carceral punch metacarpal
she sobs articular

vacuous popped viscous
she craves an ocular cavity
aqueous always humorous

double-jointed helix
she heals elliptical
hysterical licks
giggles swigs

Shock Therapy

bilateral electrode placement
short-term anaesthetic
a muscle relaxant
and salivation inhibitor

fireworks

The Good Doctor

from scarab
to scoured abdomen
scarred man
sacred care
scared

ROGUES GALLERY 3

DESTRUCTION

Darkseid

Master Antagonist

licked on lips

your plundered suns
clink, chains link

bound her
iron sings

flesh sculpts
around fists
disappointment's sheer grip

Concussion

shaken

demented pugilist
nothing cushions the blow

punch

drunk

neurofibrillary tangles
memories knot nerves

red twine
around knuckles

symptoms include: tearfulness

Bane

Life

sensitive to dissolved oxygen
taste and colour substantially changed
adversely affects filler performance
subject to excess foaming

specially formulated to the demands
of an extended shelf life

Broke

shutter chunk thoracic
sucker echolocate

perianal prick
girdle pelvic floor

sphincter kicks cloak
chokes white matter

fibrous fistula
clocks dissected loss

an incomplete injury
she loves you not

Sabretooth

the musk you muster
at the junction of groin
and adductor strain

your severed flexor
is all molar, all molten

you dig in
for balance

claw, meet pliers

needle nose to incisor

                    this crackle of root deep
                    in the jaw

your healing factor
throbbing root up

red

you swallow

MODOK

you calculate the precise angle of each touch
    each sharpshooter's wind resistance
    each analyst's taut skin
    each captive's raised hair
    each henchman's aching pore
has its axis

the warp and weft of perception
you scuttle across
my deviant spider
your brain a pair of pincers
creaking with poison

your timing is impeccable
your accuracy ruthless

Mister Sinister

Nathaniel, you've become bent
trident turned heraldic
a pronged caduceus
pin strop skin throat clotted in your blood

will you find a cure for your lip
alight with a needle stick
ease back sweet fat
as your tongue slips scalpel

each caper
a massacre
my grand mal

Kid Miracleman

half a head

sucks sulphur
unilateral and pulsating
analgesic jelly bean

stumbling aura

ion channel fires cortex
crushed glass eye
tinnitus or photophobic

visual snow

digitolingual or cheiro-oral
edema cold and moist
gelid fortified spectra (neat-o)

reversible limb

Venom

guillotine grin
glass jaw
hatchet fish
gas unnerved
bass growls bulldozer

slobbering envy
needle-tipped scorcher
your catgut strung vile
spit lavished
slug chews adrenal

tongue firmly planted in my cheek

Carnage

I have no illusions
no fat moons or narcissistic reflections

this is not about romance
            but adrenaline,
my darling glandular vampire

you don't love my face or my opinions
        rictus and libertine
        just my willingness to step into traffic
                        off ledges
the swooping   ecstatic   nausea
epinephrine surging for us both

one fat adrenoceptor
        a ravenous beak
        a sucker   for risk

always there to
            shove me
                        off a cliff

Toad

spat collusion
you thickly congeal

slick as lamprey
your speech a rasping organ

vascular plexus
throbs through my oral cavity

blade of your lamina
carves my liminal space

tympanic or salival
wetly you tear

Mephisto

Apple

the original tongue twister
forever a luscious grin

dangling every peach and diamond
    every husky whisper
    each tug of gold
deep in the belly of desire

Pitchfork

defined by tine and slit
      eyes gimlet
      pupils warped
      and narrow
every limb a blade

your words are razors
embrace a clutch of barbed wire

but there are rules
      no pleasure in tormenting the righteous
      there must be exchange, consent
      there must be a pact

you
you have to   resist

Serpent

we had a bargain!

> *wretched piss-pot*
> *boiling oil*

how dare you ascend!

Blackheart

ugliness has a way of accumulating
gathering in corners
mewling and petulant
disgust throbs to life

    heartworm
    wriggling hook
    deep intramuscular itch

he finds you whole and lovely
but with a mind made of teeth
he gnaws the softness out
   weds the bones of you

he loves what you're capable of
                     (skinned kitten)
            (oven baby)
the horror
of human
rubbed raw

Penance

after the blast turned 612 people to ash, then to spikes in your skin,
you became a tripwire to circulatory collapse, a skinflint bent on
tissue perfusion, each pierce a critical loss

the hypoxia drools down your metabolic acidosis
hypodermic drags against your eyelids
                    cellular leak

sphincters relax
guilt boils
gut septic
preganglionic nerves
                lend sympathy

Red Skull

never a victim of acid or blade
merely contraction and keratin, skin's armour

> he grins a nine iron
> dapper eclabium
> slaps against jackboots
> the rigour to my mortis

your cheekbone and orbital
slough dragon scale
islands of skin grind
against each other
bleeding tectonic plates

> my body rubble
> beneath your blitz
> my twisted rune
> you flicker heteroclitic

riding crop
a minefield

> clutch
> choke out
> see red

Mastermind

Auditory

each breath percussive
you murmur paracusia
your voice glittering fish

lesions on my brainstem
like kisses on my neck

salacious or subcortical
your whispers closer than skin to fat
your tongue flat against my brain

      tell me

tell me what to do
      the voices
tell me what to do

Proprioceptive

you nestle so deeply
    beyond the crook of elbow
             bend of neck
        flesh between fingers

you caress the anchor of each tendon
    articulate kinaesthesia
    visceral tugs and slide
    buried deep in muscle memory

my own   my organ
intimate   hand to eye

I love you haptic
fuck you   blind

Galactus

you see me as morsel
           as molecule
           so minute a delicacy
           as to barely register
               the pleasure of taste

but you must eat, my love
           it is your nature to devour
              and for my insignificance
              the smallest of suns
                 ignites my cells' engines

let me extinguish myself
           in your hunger

Omega Red

your entanglement, comrade,
heightens my value
болту́н — нахо́дка для шпио́на

your suckers interrogate
beak sharp as bottle cap
a knack for reconnaissance
        you take

scars gouge your shell
like an enraged mollusc
tendrils choke out
        you take

you embrace the toxic
wallow in inky sludge
seven-eyed, you tickle
my tentacle throat
        you take

all sphincter
all muscle

you take everything

Doomsday

snow
flood
famine
pollution
pandemic
hypercane
solar storm
cosmic dust
impact event
black hole burst
cosmic radiation
cybernetic revolt
grey goo scenario
zombie apocalypse
geomagnetic reversal
vacuum metastability event
abrupt reposition of the Earth's axis
massive flood basalt or supervolcano
nuclear, chemical or biological armageddon

Acknowledgements

My sincere thanks to Mike O'Connor, Dan Varrette and Insomniac Press for taking on *DOOM*. Special thanks to Paul Vermeersch for his keen editorial eye, encyclopedic knowledge of comic books and friendship.

Thanks to all the independent publications and literary journals that published excerpts from *DOOM*, including *dead (g)end(er)*, *Carousel*, *Broken Pencil*, rob mclennan and *The Peter F. Yacht Club*, *ditch,*, *dandelion* and *Misunderstandings Magazine*. Early versions of the very first pieces I wrote for *DOOM* were collected in the chapbook *Villains*, published in 2008 by derek beaulieu's No Press. Special thanks to *Matrix* magazine, where "Three Love Poems for Dr. Doom," the earliest incarnation of this project, appeared in issue #74 (Fan Friction).

I am lucky enough to be surrounded by the most incredible collection of creative, brilliant friends and colleagues. My thanks and love go out to everyone who read this manuscript and encouraged my work: Jonathan Ball, Chris Blais, Christian Bök (who has provided me with the most compelling example for how a poet might transform into a supervillain), Chad Bower and *About Heavy Metal*, Di Brandt, Natalee Caple, Stacey Case, Gennie Catroppa (my polarity), Olivia Catroppa (my pirate), Jason Christie, Mark Coatsworth, Dani Couture (who every day makes me feel like a superhero), Phil Creswell and *Angry Metal Guy*, Mike Crossley, Chris

Ewart, Shane Faulkner, Jon Paul Fiorentino and Snare Books, ryan fitzpatrick, Stacey May Fowles, Rachel Hopwood and everyone at *Now Hear This!* and *Descant*, Jim Johnstone, James Keast and all the folks at *Exclaim!*, Bill Kennedy, Ian Kinney, Sandy Lam, Thérèse Lanz, Cassius Leipert, Imogen Leipert, Jeremy Leipert, Emily McDowall (my oldest friend and healer), Nicole Markotić, Colin Martin, Melinda Mattos, Sachiko Murakami, Desirée Ossandon and everyone at *Canada Arts Connect*, Sean Palmerston and *Hellbound*, Panic (Heather Cromarty), Krista Pettipas, Sina Queyras, angela rawlings, Andrea Ryer, Kacy Sawchuck, Emily Schultz, Jordan Scott, Summer Kalbfleisch-Scott, the Vilipend boys, David Ward, Georgia Webber, Raymond Westland and *Alternative Matter*, Darren Wershler, Darryl Whetter, Adam Wills, Julie Wilson, Emma Woolley and Liz Worth. Thanks to the organizers of the A B Series, the Scream, Pivot, AvantGarden and livewords, and to Pages Books on Kensington, McNally Robinson, Pages Books (Toronto) and Type Books.

Thanks to the peerlessly talented, endlessly positive and indefatigable Evan Munday, whose illustrations grace the pages of *DOOM*. Evan has produced many pieces based on *DOOM*, including pin-up calendars and Valentine's cards, as well as the pieces in the book. He has been a joy to work with, and his ability to draw supervillains in assless chaps is a gift unmatched in contemporary illustration.

My love and thanks to my mate, Christopher

Gramlich, who has taught me the true meaning of loyalty. A brilliant editor, he challenges me to become a better writer every day; a fiercely devoted partner, he challenges me to become a better person every day. He has never let me settle for anything but perfection in my work, and his contribution to this book cannot be overstated.

From the very outset and at every turn, my family has supported my creative work and loved me despite my strangeness. Thanks to Margaret Walschots, Harry Walschots, Michael Walschots, Gerarda Walschots (RIP), Ronald Pazik (RIP) and Zina Mihailovsky for their generosity and unconditional love. Thanks to my aunts, uncles and cousins, and all the wonderful people in my life I call my aunts and uncles and cousins regardless of blood ties. I love you all.

The process of writing *DOOM* has been much more than an exercise in villainy. Over the past four years, the generous, brilliant people who populate my life have demonstrated their heroism in innumerable ways. Thank you, my friends and acquaintances, pen pals and Twitter friends, band members and fellow music writers, colleagues and partners in crime. When my terrible plans all come to fruition and the world is at last mine, I will not fail to remember and honour your kindness.